The Pathophysiology Of Longing

By

Joanna Acevedo

Black Centipede Press

Black Centipede Press
Denver, CO
blackcentipedepress@gmail.com

ISBN #: 978-1-7353275-1-8
Cover Art: Anne Finkelstein
Design and layout: Anne Finkelstein
Copyright:2020

Acknowledgements
Thanks to the editors of the following journals who have previously published my poems.

"religion question" appeared in *Lychee Rind* and appeared again in *Black Fox Literary Journal* in Summer 2020.

"Don't Call It A Comeback" appeared in *Black Fox Literary Journal* in Summer 2020.

"God Poem" appeared in *io literary journal* in Summer 2020.

Special thanks to the following people:

Thank you to Anne Finkelstein, James Acevedo, Anna Kampfe, Nora Goodbody, Skye Baptiste, Plum Champlin, Elliott Sky Case, Bernard Ferguson, Joshua Furst, Jeffrey Eugenides, Michael Everett, the students at the NYU Creative Writer's House 2019-2020, and lastly to Brady Flanigan, without whom there would be no book.

For Brady, who is more than a footnote in someone else's book.

Table Of Contents
Part One: Prodrome
do you think of me - 9
vicious - 10
I'm not myself when I'm with you - 12
fire - 13
inside the inside of the beast - 13
this body - 17
the distance that exists between all people - 19
that which is front of us is also behind us - 20
the golden hour - 21
beauty can manifest itself in many forms - 22
i need help immediately - 24
a gun is a weapon - 25
religion question - 26
a man's hand on a woman's thigh - 27
i eat desire for breakfast - 29
Untitled IV - 30

Part Two: Mania
Don't Call It A Comeback - 32
Before The Magic Runs Out - 33
The Pathophysiology of Longing - 35
Desire is an action - 37
Not only will this kill you, it will hurt the whole time you're dying - 38
Ode to Atypical Antipsychotics - 40
God Poem - 41
Fragments II - 42
Assorted Hopes and Dreams - 44
Obsession - 45

'Tis the wound of love goes home - 47
Manic Fatigue - 48
Can You Think Of Something You Don't Have Words For Yet? - 49
Want, a Breakdown - 50
Assorted Questions - 51

Part Three: Depression
Loss (noun): the fact or process of losing something or someone - 54
Smoke - 55
the philosophical implications of two-ness - 56
whiplash - 58
Untitled III - 59
Thank You Poem - 60
13hrs, 43mn - 61
Late Nights - 63
Prose Poem - 64
In a strictly theoretical manner of speaking - 66
the last smoking holdouts - 67
nudes - 68
Proceed at your own risk - 69
cough - 70
free association - 72

Part Four: Acceptance
Fragments - 74
gift poem - 76
poem to be burned - 78
this modern psychosis - 79
sunburnt - 81
all i have to offer is my own confusion - 82

Poked-Faced - 83

existence is too enormous - 84

Banging your head against a wall for one hour burns 150 calories - 86

Inertia - 87

on not loving you - 88

there will be blood - 89

What is fear afraid of? - 90

smoking poem - 91

light a match - 92

Part One: Prodrome
Relating to or denoting the period between the appearance of initial symptoms and the full development of a rash or fever.

"What's madness but nobility of soul
At odds with circumstance?"
— "In A Dark Time," Theodore Roethke

do you think of me
i want for nothing, no
       i want nothing
the release that comes with sleep
           with your arm around me and the heat of outside
                  beaten back/

i want to be back in that cold room
       the blinds drawn

and your voice on the phone, it lulls me

do you think of me? in those odd moments
       between sleep/and/wake
"what would make you feel better?" he asks

       time
       i say

vicious
early, the light is vicious.
it cuts into me and you—
and i know my history, guns drawn
along the avenue, i call you
some nights, you come down
from your perch to torment me.
i know you so well, if you were here
right now, you'd be bullying me
for drags of my marlboro,
calling me a coal-miner,
your belt buckle glinting
in the red glow of neon. this ain't
west virginia.
i wear dresses now.

penny for your thoughts
and you want me to try your
back-porch moonshine, i bet
it tastes like the bead
of sweat on your lower lip
i bet it tastes like the last girlfriend
you had before me, the one
whose name i'll never know.
you want me to bend over
face down for you.
you want me to laugh at
your jokes. you want me
to make you laugh. funny, isn't it
that you never ask me

in the loose time and space
before you say, "i guess
i'll be going,"
what i could possibly want—

I'm not myself when I'm with you
I roll around on the bed trying to get you   to roll around   with me.
          You make a point   of subduing me with hands and words.
We make plans
to rob banks,
honey in the water,
a cigarette dipped
in ash.
I feel I am capable of more   when I am with you.
This is not necessarily   a good thing.
More what?   More violence—
to myself,   certainly   and maybe other people.
More cruelty.
I keep my voice clipped,   tap my cigarette on the table.   Look
out the window at the pigeons. They seem so carefree.   Not like us,
Alone in this small room,   fighting each other.

I wish I could pin down exactly how you make me feel. Less than
what I was before.   A maximum sum   of lesser parts.
A throb of pressure.
A hangover that lasts   and persists into the afternoon. I curl my hair,
pour salt in the wound come back to you   with my hands open
like the Madonna.
The ice melts in the glass.   I melt   in your arms
          into something else. Something worse.

fire

something sexy about your thumb moving up and down on the glass.
light a match
and watch it burn—phosphorus leanback.
believing you is not a habit i've practiced.
i lie on the bed wanting you to take my makeup off

with your tongue.

later, i realize i don't remember the color of your eyes.
in your arms, i become superfluous. a bit of flesh
between your fingers.

i only almost wanted you. in photographs, you prove yourself with metal
and blood. the same tools of war that men
greater than you have used
for generations
now rest in your capable hands. i can't deny that i am attracted to the
smell of gunpowder.
i don't want to want
violence.

on the phone, i explain my desire
for bruises. you tell me you understand, sympathize—
but we can't act on our wants for geographical reasons.

my needs are secondary
to how your lips move when you hurt me. fire is secondary
to the way it burns down everything in its path. trusting you is not a habit
i've practiced. the match flickers in your palm

and goes out. a chemical trick
of the light—

inside the inside of the beast
i want passion. a terrifying thing to want
or need — i find melodrama seductive.
i find myself manipulative   — carrying
over last week's sadness into this week's
epiphanies. emily said "Pain — has an
Element of Blank" — and i believe it,
i see myself as a mirror for your insecurities,
my terror. i do not want to be held, just
held accountable — for my actions.
could you handle it? if you were here —
i wonder sometimes. a look inside the inside
of the beast.

sometimes i feel like the destroyer of worlds.
i contain multiplicities — there is a me
inside of me who does not love you — who
does not need to do this. who does need to
lie prostrate — on the rocks. she is screaming.
stop this, she says. *this self-torture — it's
unattractive.* how does one talk to oneself?
i answer me with poems, free verse. try though
i do, i cannot trust my instincts.

kurt said, "I miss the comfort in being sad."
 i don't agree, and have the scars to prove it —
and yet i fear that when we see each other,
i will be something else entirely. someone you
won't like. missing you has done strange things
to me. i am a new creature — not the one

you knew and loved. i have nearly forgotten
the taste of your tongue — the feel of your chest
underneath my palms. when you come back —
will you like what you find?
or something else?

this body
this body has carried me across countries. it knows
        things i do not know.
                it knows what it felt like
        to lie with you on sheets that were possibly
less-than-clean.
        how close is close?
                when time and space separate us
i have memories. years of self-abuse have rendered my brain
        full of holes. but the body
remembers.

it knows how it felt to have your hip bone pinning me down
        like an anchor.
               that kiss like a gun
a surprise
        tasting of cigarettes and miller high
                life.
        i wish i had your face next to mine on the bed now
but you are cities away. what i have
                is this.

this body knows. it remembers what heart and mind
        cannot.
                i know what i know. i know what distance
tastes like.
        it tastes empty—like rainwater
                like your skin after a long time
underground. in the parking lot
        of my mind

i wait. for the door to open, and you to come rushing through.
    you do not come. i wonder how long it will be before i see you next. there are no answers
    for these kinds of questions.
i will wait for as long as this body allows me to wait.

the distance that exists between all people
you left his house at four in the morning, because he had someone else coming over,
      someone whose name you'll never know. you didn't ask
too many questions for fear that he would catch on to your immediate obsession with him,
      with the sheets on his bed, with the cheap beer
 he poured down his throat—in fits of brilliance—the newports he smoked;
      the tiny details you would remember for years to come.
his face was planar and complicated, his voice a rasp from smoking and screaming;
       humanity was too kind a word. you walked home drunk
wandering down streets that were familiar and yet not, past the twenty-four hour
      dentist's office and the bodegas and the laundromats
still operating despite the cover of night. when you got home you undressed and felt
      the bruises he had left on your skin, the bite marks
on your neck. there was a degree of necessity. it meant, *you are here i am here.*
      you felt purposeful in his hands. a hollow object,
meant to be filled. later, you would find that you needed him, not just for the feeling
      of necessity but also because you needed someone
to see you, he saw you. why him? don't worry, he said of the vast distance between you,
      the distance that exists between all people. together,
                he said, we'll close it.

that which is behind us is also in front of us
      for Michael Everett

long walks, trailing smoke, we are all alone together in the grand scheme of things — i ask *how could you* in the bleak morning light you smoke your cigarette in florida and wonder what i'm talking about — and i'm a sucker for punishment

you ask me to resend the document — i tell you it contains all of our secrets it's no wonder you can't see them
and i was always going to be like this, did you know
in siberia, you can light the snow on fire?

i pick things out of my hair

and you don't call me, i don't know why i thought you would, i miss you but also i wish that you were here, in my small room with me at the end of
the known universe — i wish you got locked up for what you did

the small ceramic cats, the blood on my thumbs, the white on the sheets, the loose cigarettes, the range rovers and SUVs, the modest mouse on the CD player
the cold coffee out on the stoop

i never thought there would be an ending, but never thought the beginning would feel like this — we are always in motion, calmly dialing our mothers who want nothing more than for us to come home to them — we never will

the golden hour
we are almost limitless. all of this could be yours, he says
    with a sweep of his arm.
i am putting a cold compress on my forehead. i do not want to want
    anything. i want a month of tuesdays, a song that never ends.

today i am vulnerable. feeling lonely
    has become a way of being. i count out the days on one hand;
the other keeps time. you are trying to make me angry.
    sometimes it works.
i keep it cold and save it for when it rains.

the scars have mostly healed. i want to show you
    what they look like
        but when i go to turn the page, nothing happens.
the light touches everything. they call this "the golden hour." i call it
    tragic. usually i don't fall for your tricks. today
        is special, i guess.

beauty can manifest itself in many forms
    For Brady
he isn't blind to the wickedness of his tools, he says.
    but he's killed things. i don't think that parakeet is going to

hell

he says. mid-may, and i can't stand to wear pants for one more day. i want to kill spring
watch it die with my arrow in its back.
    instead, sitting inside, he reminds me i have not yet begun to defile myself. anything can represent itself as a piece of beauty

    he says. even me? i want to ask—
and don't, stupid child.

you need to back the right horse. i've wasted all my chips
    on him, he doesn't even want me.
    what do you get out of these fevered conversations? i want to know.
for i am
    fractured. our unlikely friendship scatters like roaches when i drink too many beers.

    i'm not complaining, just observing. he puts up with me, mean drunk though i am—
    beauty can manifest itself in many forms. he appeals
    to my baser tendencies.

    we are corrupting each other, slowly but surely, the way water corrupts a disc.

i need help immediately
they say this is the coldest spring on record
in 42 years. i live in a cage without walls
and make assorted prayers.
cut the limb off the tree before it rots.
i need help immediately.

on better days, i take long walks and we talk
about the semipermanent changes
we have made to our own bodies.
nothing lasts forever, but i like to believe
 we are making lasting impressions
on each other, like fingerprints
on dough.

i have nothing left to give you:
a book with your name, an argument that will not be settled easily,
4.8 liters of blood.
i shed my skin like a lizard as if by doing so
i could rid myself
of the need for you.

i will never be free of you. five years,
a procession of badly lit bars,
a wine bottle
opened with a knife.
you speak my language now.
i sit alone in the cold, shivering.

a gun is a weapon
a gun is a weapon in the same way that a fist is a weapon way that a kiss is a weapon a kiss is a weapon in the same way that a crush is a weapon a crush is a gun in the same way that my crushes are always smoking a kiss can be hard or soft in the same way a fist can be hard or soft *do you have to know a person's history to know a person?* a gun is a weapon in the same way that you are a weapon your face is a razor your hands are bullets your tongue is a gun which is a weapon in the same way that a fist is a weapon and the same way that a kiss is a weapon when used appropriately which is really a way to say that it should be used sparingly, if at all a crush is a weapon when it is smoking which is always and wearing that denim jacket which i've always loved a gun is a weapon it can be hard or soft like a fist or a kiss or a crush or a razor or bullets *my history is none of your business.*

religion question
my religion is your ribcage.
        i come to your body to worship. at the altar
of your hip bone
        i hang myself. *do you want me
too?* you are a phantom limb
        that still aches.

it is blasphemous
        to want someone this much.
i wait, counting days like two-faced coins.
        someday, possibly soon
you will drip back into my life,
        a leaky faucet of desire run dry
from too much wanting.

you are church, priest, prayer.
        i click rosary beads together
on the face of your photograph. my wrists
        want to be underneath your wrists.
do you want me too?
        you are the pause between hard questions.

a man's hand on a woman's thigh
what was once power
        is now leaking through my fingers.
a man's hand on a woman's thigh
        looks like a promise. what do we see
when we see other
        people? i have more questions
                than answers. i turn the same
ideas over and over
                like marbles. i do not find
release.

i know if you looked, you would find yourself
        between these words. a man's hand
on a woman's hand
        looks like a threat.
                search for yourself
among these pages. i don't know if you're like
        what you find there. what do we see
                when we see
        ourselves?

there is so much i simply
        do not know
about wanting you. a man's hand
                on a woman's back
                      looks like an offering.
        every day a new surprise of mood—
a new torture at the hands
        of distance.

i cannot protect myself
       from myself. i fear i am destined
              to roam the earth, wanting.
always fitting myself
              into your footsteps.
     what do we see
when we see each other? a mirror of desire,
       a last look at your face in the dark.

i eat desire for breakfast
    for Bernard Ferguson
hold me or hold me down. want me or don't. hurt me
    with your hands like knives, hands i have never loved
but have wanted every night for the past five years. i don't lie
    but i have wanted to lie with you. i think of you
in the loosest parts of the night, when the darkness rubs its face
    against the edge of the sky, when i am about to fall asleep. last march
i sat on your bed and waited for you to come and sit beside me, the heat of the room
    cooking us both. you undressed me. i slid you out of your sweat-stained t-shirt.
i put my hands on your shoulders,
    felt your solidness underneath my fingertips.
you warned me not to leave any lasting marks.
    even now i want you, if only to remind me that we are real, that
we have bodies, that our bodies can touch
    even for a moment. you moved me the way you wanted me,
a doll with arms and legs. i bent and changed under your hands. i have never been
    so happy. with your hands like knives, or possibly bullets
you touched me. now i burn with it. i eat desire for breakfast.
    i want you to bruise, to bleed, to hurt me
to break me into the pieces i was made out of. i want you to leave
    lasting marks.

Untitled IV
my red hands leave their mark on you.
you held me like i was something worth holding—
a vial full of gold, a barrel of snakes. careful;
you laid me down on my back.
i closed my eyes so i would not forget.

remembering now feels like pulling teeth.
your absence gapes loud and heavy in the room.
i can still feel the quality of space that you left.

my knees twist and ache. my skin blisters. without you—
i am lost within myself. i wander in and out
of memory. you pulled my hair, wrenched my head back.
the pain felt pure, like truth.

now i have nothing to offer except the dirt
under my nails, the blood
under my skin. you took from me
the smallest parts
of myself. i want you to come back.
i want you to take more.
i want you to take all of it.

Part Two: Mania

Mania, also known as manic syndrome, is a state of abnormally elevated arousal, affect, and energy level, or "a state of heightened overall activation with enhanced affective expression together with lability of affect."

"Aren't all love stories, at their core, great mistakes?" — "To the Guanacos at the Syracuse Zoo," Chen Chen

"Desire makes beggars out of each and every one of us." — "Phom Penh Diptych: Wet Season," Jenny Xie

Don't Call It A Comeback
I ration myself out like milk in coffee,
A little at a time. A month's budget of sweetness expended
In a tongue's trip, a slip
Of the heart. You are coming back,
October you say. I still remember how I almost loved
Your violence. In that room above the street, on Melrose
Your dog nosed my thighs. I smoked a Marlboro
Into an empty beer can. You explained to me
The blues.

He says he misses me,
In the way it's just a little bit fun
To see how much throttle you're willing to give the car
Once you pull out onto the road.
He says it in a way that makes me think
It's not a compliment.

The chemical taste in the back of my throat
Reminds me of you. In your grip, I am reduced
To my basest desires, a sex object
With arms and legs. I struggle to reclaim my grasp
On needs and wants. When you come back—
What will happen? I'm not sure
I really want to know.

Before The Magic Runs Out
Early mornings, still asleep, I achieve brilliance
Coffee slick lips chasing cigarette butts
A bad taste—of loss—that follows me throughout the day.

And I am alone, both literally and spiritually
With a headache and a stomachache and a need
For new things.

I don't save my work. I prefer to leave it up
To the universe to decide what sticks
And what doesn't. I placate myself with red wine in coffee mugs,
Bacardi in stolen glasses, tequila mixed with ginger ale.
The flies buzz outside my room. Once in a while
One of them makes it inside. I kill it
With a roll of rolled up
Newspaper.

There is peace in solitude. There are also nerves,
A fear that comes from not knowing
When I will see you next. When I will lie on my back
With your head on my chest, stroking
Your hair. Some memories I treasure
More than others.

You say that when we see each other, it will be all the better
Because we will have waited. I want to believe you,
The way I want to believe in magic. In my dreams
You hold me down and I am contained, finally. I hope,
For better or worse—

We see each other before the magic runs out.

The Pathophysiology Of Longing
Loose cannons never slept so well at night. Late April, I become aware
Of the passage of time. I have been living in an altered state; you are in another state
And I cannot find you, though I look through old books, old paragraphs
Of free verse with your name hidden in between the syllables. I have become
Like a child, tapping my foot against the floor in the hopes
Of summoning you like a demon,
As if the right configuration of taps will make you appear
In all your ruddy glory, belly hanging slightly over your belt buckle. I know
This is not the case. I cannot will you into existence with sage brushes
And poems. I lie on my back so I will have strange dreams
Instead.

There are limits to what I can do
With my short legs. You never seemed to mind
My causal limitations. I wonder if it is warmer where you are, if you are happier
Sticking to your guns; literally and figuratively. I gave to you
What was not mine to give—my kinesthesia, my stone-cold heart. You turned me down
With a laugh-cough and said there were more important things than love.
I wanted to believe you. Sometimes I still do.

Keys palmed and security guards charmed, I know that some disruptions
Will resolve themselves. A ripple in time, a piece of turbulence
You are a disturbance that must be smoothed. I run my hands over my thighs.

I see our future as a spool, a forward motion, a rolling wave.
You keep me at arm's length. If I could
I would walk across the blood-brain barrier that separates us; tracing capillaries
And veins across the cold of your chest. I think it's impossible
To be close to another person. What will come next?
There is nothing to do but wait.

Desire is an action

Desire is an action. I light a small fire at the end of your name. Why do men insist
        On proving their violence?
You spend too much time showing me your gun collection.
        I have photos of you with rifles, bayonets.   Part of me is glad
You are capable of taking care of yourself. The other part
        Wants you to be soft.
I ask questions, write letters from across the country
        That will never be sent.   Who is responsible
For the end of the world? I cross myself off the list.
        You say coolly
That we are no longer the people we used to be.   Why not? I want to know.
        I don't know, you say. I wish I had the answers. I don't.

Healing is a process. Everyone says
        It takes time to feel right again. I have nothing
But time.
        I wish you would have swallowed me whole.   Instead I exist in pieces,
Ragged chunks. In your bedroom, I told you the truth
        And you disbelieved me. Now I crow   I-told-you-so
From my perch at the top of the universe. We are far apart.
        Miles separate us. I want to close the distance with paper dreams
And smoke screens and wishes.
        You cannot escape longing.   No matter how far you run
There will always be wanting.   No matter how much you have
        There will always be a switchblade, sliding open.

Not only will this kill you, it will hurt the whole time you're dying
Why do we want? In May, I run out of responsibilities,
    Free-falling. Time has lost its meaning. The days bleed together. I can feel us
Starting up again. Maybe we never stopped. I know you're scared—I am too. I see two
Dead birds on my walk—a bad omen. I am starting to believe in God again, another
    Bad sign. The last time this happened, they locked me up,
    Threw away the key. It took all of my wits to get me out.
That happens, you say. If you're not careful.

I don't know how to be careful. You are cavalier. I kiss someone else
    For something to do. I don't mention this. Likely you are doing the same thing.
We are solitary beings these days, moving in solitary orbits. Like ships in the night.
    I light my lantern, wait for you to pass so I can signal that I am here—
    Are you here, too?
    I wait for a light in the darkness. There it is.
    A small glow, a pool of yellow in the black. Your voice on the phone like a blade
In the morning. I toss the scissors away, lock the doors, turn off the lamp. Make myself
As safe as I can stand. Safety in numbers, they say. Are you numbered, too?

I worry you are disappearing. Distance takes something away from us, as usual. I try

To hold onto the edges of the square with my fingertips. You are working hard
On your own projects. There is nothing left for me to do but wait for the space to close,
For the doors to shut. I move from second to second, wanting.
I am a live wire. You are the nail, a second before the hammer hits it.

Ode to Atypical Antipsychotics

Say you want me. Say there is a time and a place for everything. Say you need me.
    Say the sun sets in the West. Say atypical antipsychotic.
Say crazy, but not crazy-crazy. Say you know what I'm talking about.

I want you on your back or on your front or on your side. I want you upside down
    And laughing with your heels in the air. I want you smiling for the camera,
Driving one-handed on the bridge, smoking a Hotrod cigarette. I want you
    To be crazy about me. I want you to laugh and laugh and laugh.

Now what I have the most of is silence. I can hold it in my hands
    Bottle it, sell it. I take pills to keep it quiet. Say lithium. Say locked ward.
Say you won't regret it.

I want you spread-eagled on the blacktop. I want you shouting at the top of your lungs.
    I want you running so fast not even the Devil can catch you. I want you to tell me Something you've never told anyone else. Say secret. Say promise.
    Say mood stabilizer. Say I-told-you-so.

I keep my emotions in a jar and take them out when I need to use them. I don't know
    How to be any other way. Say steel cube. Say box-cutter knife.
Say cut me a window. Say make me an opening. Say set me free.

God Poem

I want to see what God sees. Do you think He
Plays games or just
Watches? Mid-afternoon, I think about the nature
Of violence. The light is no longer
Coming in through the blinds. I wait for your call—
A last look at the inside of the inside. The satisfying crunch
Of knuckles against bone. I have never been in a fight,
Only feared for my life on strange, blank occasions
But I have wanted to hurt you.

You tell me I've made an appearance
In your nightmares. This is more or less
Flattering. I want to look into the face of God, ask Him
The same questions I ask you. You want to be significant. The world
Aches with your significance. Tools of desire become tools of war
In your hands. Do you think He likes it
When we argue about small things? I want to know
What God knows. A little about
Everything.

How do you plan for uncertainty? For tragedy? For
A car speeding down the road, for saying your name out loud,
For the fire that it elicits? How does God know
When to stop? When does he say, alright,
I've had enough? Can he even say that?
I want to see what God sees.

Fragments II
1.
I ask for forgiveness. A fever dream, a birdsong, a lipstick print on the face of the unknown. The future is uncertain; I try to piece together the fragments. You say you'll try your best to maintain the status quo. I thank God for these little allowances.

2.
Mornings, I extract myself from the sticky terror of sleep. I only dream about you sometimes. It is never pleasant to wake up and find that you are not here, you are only a memory. But I need to sleep, I need a reason to get from morning to night time.

3.
I talk to God on Wednesdays. The doctors have a name for this. I ignore them; what do they know? I am on edge mostly. Roethke said, "The edge is what I have." I see what he means. Being on edge is a way of being, a state of mind, an altered consciousness. There are good and bad things about this: both pros and cons.

4.
From my heightened point, I thought I knew more than other people. Now I know that this was a delusion. You remark that I seem to be doing well. It astounds me, the way I fool people—but perhaps you are just not looking closely enough. We've never scrutinized each other—maybe we should start.

5.
Suddenly, you presume shyness. After all we've been through together? I ask, with the tip of my thumb bleeding in my mouth. I want you to share:

I want to crack you open like an egg and see what is inside. You will never consent to this. Oh well. I go back to my books.

Assorted Hopes and Dreams
I hope that when I grow up I'm nothing like myself. I hope that you don't get to know me. He says: you're too young to be this angry. Every seven years, our cells are completely replaced with new ones. I hope that I meet lots of nice concrete in the city. I hope that when you meet me for the last time, you know it's the last time, and you're especially mean to me. That would be a nice change of pace. I hope that when I have children, they pretend they don't know me at social functions. I hope that I miss you so much that I actually conjure you into existence, like summoning a demon. I will make lots of nice sacrifices to God, or to Satan, whoever calls me back first. I hope I remember to call my dad back. I hope that when you come back, you recognize me. I hope I've changed a lot. I hope I've done some real soul-searching, and had some major Revelations. I hope when you see me, you still like me. I want you to kiss me like we're in the movies, with music swelling in the background, and then we'll run off into the sunset together. I want it to always be sunset. I want the sun to always be setting.

Obsession
Sunday night, I use my Get Out Of Jail Free card.
Touch-starved, looking for meaning in between the lines
Of the things you say to me, secret messages in the songs
You say are stuck in your head, I know
I am obsessing. How could I not?
When I have been alone
Two months, a far cry
From your arms. You have never shown me
Any amount of mercy. Reason is no excuse. I can feel you
Pulling closer, our mutual hysteria
Bubbling and boiling. Do you think of me?
In the space between morning and night,
The dark-light of insomnia close and clutching. Do you want
The way I want?

Manic, I feel no guilt
For my actions. What am I guilty of? Of thinking too much,
Moving my hands down my thighs, finding my ankles still attached
To my feet. Some days, I think I can levitate. Other days,
I find myself firmly planted on the floor. You say I'm doing well—
What do you know? You do not live in this body, you do not
Understand its flights
And falls.

Obsession is a taste in the mouth, a flavor on the tongue,
A thrum in the blood. It feels good
To think these same thoughts again after a long day
Of doing nothing. I am afraid
You will catch on, sound the alarm,

Call fire in the lighthouse. But for tonight,
The dog sleeps soundly at your feet. All is well
In Hell, Wild Turkey and terrible *heat*.

'Tis the wound of love goes home!
1. Whenever you breathe out, I breathe in.
2. I am the skinned rabbit bouncing against a thigh, I have died seven times at your hands and plan to come back for more deaths when you come back from down South.
3. Why won't you come back from down South?
4. I'm on a first-name basis with God, my name signed in someone else's' blood.
5. A little bit of cruelty goes a long way.
6. I fear I am overcompensating; it's not that I'm afraid of you, it's that I'm afraid of what you'll do next.
7. What is your tolerance to pain?
8. A brand into the flesh, a bite mark, a bruise, a red leather pair of handcuffs, a smoke screen made of Japanese paper and the same tapestry I stared at for almost two years.
9. I am a person, no matter how small.

Manic Fatigue
I am whatever you have hidden under your mattress. I heave fistfuls of ash from under your bed. I am the taste of pavement, seconds before the car comes. I am the siren in the dark, signaling that something has gone terribly, terribly wrong. I am the bump in the night. I am falling from your fifth floor window, I am jumping out of your moving car. I am your nightmare, I am the mad run from the bathroom to the bed.

There is no reason why you should be afraid of me.
I would never do anything to hurt you.

I am the bird call, the smoke signal, the curve in the highway that you are sure you are going to spin off of and tumble down into the brambles. I am dangerous. This body knows things it shouldn't, it knows how to kill and how to bring back to life. I am the skinned rabbit, the jumping off point, the place in the woods your mother told you not to go, never to go. I am the place where lost things go, keys and socks and left shoes.

I have never wanted you as much as I want you now.
It scares me.

Teach me about dying. Teach me about God, about mysteries, about the fish that live at the bottom of the ocean and never see the light. Teach me about darkness. Teach me how to see. Teach me how to want, how to feel, how to reach out for you in the middle of the night, when you've had too many whiskies and I've had too many beers. I am always, always reaching.

Can You Think Of Something You Don't Have Words For Yet?
What you are is mostly irrelevant. I have become a conduit. Say, what is the approximate condition of your wishbone? I am hips and stomach and thighs and not much else. Bodies are somehow superfluous to what is inside of us. What *is* inside of us? If you could be any type of explosion, what type would you be? Beauty walks among us. What you are is usually difficult for me to describe. Delicacy is all well and good until it breaks. Were you born this way, or did it come later, like a bad tooth that's just beginning to turn? Please turn off the coffee maker. I have become very wise in my new skin. Say, what are you doing with all those feathers?

In the beginning, there was you and me and there was nothing. I expected you to take flight; you stayed firmly planted on the ground. I have never expected much from you; maybe that was my first mistake. You erased all the bite marks with a sweep of your hand. I have become a synapse. Have you always been this disagreeable? What you are is something out of a storybook, a promise never kept, a lost key to a locked door. Tell me, what is the absolute truth behind your name? I've always wanted more: there is never enough.

Want, a Breakdown

To want is to choose. I choose to light a fire at the end of the tunnel, to create my own light. I stand with my back against the wall, your firing squad aiming their weapons. I make my own history.

To want is to donate. I give to you the veins in my calves, the gap in my teeth, the static in my head. I ash my cigarette onto your skin and watch the burn pattern grow. Lately, I have learned that yellow ink does not stay well in the skin.

To want is to have. I want to possess you the way a demon would. I want to slip underneath your face and make it move of my own accord. You see me as a curiosity, an annoyance, something to be held and then thrown away. I allow you these allowances.

To want is to need. You have quickly become indispensable. The scars on my thighs remind me what happens when a person or item becomes too important, too fast. These days, scars are all I have.

To want is to hold. You held me like I was made of precious metal and you had no regard for expensive things. Sometimes there's nothing you can do. I tighten the noose around my own neck.

Assorted Questions

Do you remember my pedigree? How often, would you say, in an average week, do you lucid dream? Do you consider yourself to be a modern cowboy? Would you please answer your phone? Are you thinking about me? What was your name again, I forget? How do you feel, specifically, about D.H. Lawrence?

What is your opinion on psychotropic drugs? On the people who take them? What are three ways you could easily improve your life? Mine? How can I make this easier for you? Do you want to go back outside? How easy would it be for you to replace me?

Do you still eat meat? Do you feel any way about that? What are you thinking about right now? What is your opinion on entropy? Do you want to get out of here? Would you follow me anywhere, or just here? What is the current state of your ego?

Do you enjoy hallucinogens? Would you, if asked, kill someone? Do you think you could take a life if need be? Do you consider yourself a great conversationalist? What is your favorite color? Is it possible to ever really be close to another human being? How does a person get to know another person? Do you miss me? Do I appear in your dreams?

What are your thoughts on jackhammer noise? Background noise? Background radiation? Do you enjoy sitting in the sun, or do you get burned easily? What's more important, the questions or the answers? Would you ever get a tattoo? Do you love me?

Are you capable of greater understanding? What are the philosophical implications of madness? Do you want to leave? Or stay? Do you like long drives? Highways? Are you on friendly terms with your subconscious? Do your feet hurt? What's more important, the journey, or the destination? What is the precise location of truth?

Part Three: Depression

A mental health disorder characterized by persistently depressed mood or loss of interest in activities, causing significant impairment in daily life.

"How does distance look?' is a simple direct question. It extends from a spaceless within to the edge of what can be loved." —*Autobiography of Red*, Anne Carson

Loss (noun): the fact or process of losing something or someone
You are not gone, you are simply misplaced.
I am getting restless. You are getting restless.
Long drives, I send you poems, you tell me you aren't trying to argue
With me. *Yes, you like me too.*
I wonder how hard it would be to drive you away permanently
With my varied neuroses. My name alive in your mouth
a fresh hell when we argue about old machinery over video chat. I have
forgotten how much I need your voice in my ears, telling me that the
universe is random and unpredictable. I love it the sense-memory of
your hands on my wrists holding me down baiting me with barbs
and bricks through the window; when I quote Baudelaire you deplore me.
We are separated by more than distance which you like
for its melodramatic qualities. Last winter I kissed your neck outside of
that bar and you told me I was being childish. I've never
laughed so much. Now we take days off from each other.
Too much too quickly is its own kind of bad medicine. I worry that we
will forget how to be friends. Another casualty of space. It's
become hard to reconcile what has changed: my face without makeup
your new beard my books your bullets. You promise me we
will stay close, despite the physical limits. Together, we are making
something new, something just for us. I just don't know what,
yet.

Smoke
You tell me to be brave.
Be braver.　　　I don't know
How to be anything more than this.　　　This body
Knows more than it lets on.　　Many, if not all
Of my wounds are self-inflicted.　　　　　　Don't worry,
He said, speeding toward　　　　　the end of the world.
Now, as things are starting to reopen—
I count time like beads, minutes and hours
Smacking away on my abacus.　　Surround myself
With small comforts.　　His voice on the phone—
A drug. How can you be close　　when you are
Far away?　　　We don't talk about the truth—
That regardless of circumstance,　　　　　we are separate.
Never hangs in the air like the sound　　after
Violence.　　　Still, I hang on with both hands,
Hoping that somehow, I will make something
Out of nothing, like trying to grab on
To smoke.

the philosophical implications of two-ness
twenty-three, and i think i've already met all the people
    i'll ever need to. you don't tell me her name,
but what i want to know is:
    what does she have that i don't?
    i say, it takes a village, rinse my face
with cold water. i know that we need
    more than each other, especially
when space separates us. i try not to let it
    bother me.
    but it does.

how can we be more than two things?
    a poet and a drunk. you contemplate the philosophical
implications of two-ness with me,
    late nights. once you told me
you needed to do it with someone else
    for the change of pace. i pretended the thought of you
with someone else
    didn't hurt me. i do not want you,
but i want you. in your arms, i am one thing: a body—
    what you call
    a mutually beneficial relationship.

i wish i could translate all of my feelings
    into lines like this.
    this is what the ancients called: impossible.
    we are not a pair
    but we are, somehow, together, across distance.
these days, i crave the clarity of summer,

counting down the days
      and months
            til you come back.

whiplash
the world acts upon me for mysterious reasons. sunday morning, i struggle to reclaim
my lost brilliance. sounds have lost their sound. and i am underwater, swimming towards the light.

i have fallen so far, so fast
i have whiplash. you tell me i'm doing well. i wonder how you have come to that conclusion. i miss your face, miss your voice, miss lying on your chest listening
to your heart beat out my name in between beats. when we started
did you ever think
it would come to this?

my short-circuiting brain compliments your complaints. we are an odd pair.
in the fog, i look for the lighthouse.
i know better than to look to you for salvation. instead
i crawl into the eye of the storm,
hunker down,
wait for the thunder to pass.

Untitled III

antipsychotic fog, and my mind is as blank and white
as a sheet of paper. i can hear your voice through the trees, hushing me
warning me about incompatibilities. i try not to want you;
you are in my blood like a poison. like a balloon
i expand and contract, becoming more and more beautiful
with each breath. halogen knows, halogen explodes.
and i am fundamentally incapable of stillness,
a champagne cork spilling out into your palms;
you do not want me, but you want me.
you mention in passing that maybe i have a problem,
and maybe, i do. its name is
your name, its face is gold and green and reflects upon the state
of the universe.

a philosopher's stone unturns you. mercury in your blood;
you look to mythology for answers—
there are none. i look to medicine;
it leaves me disoriented and wanting. there is no cure for what i have.
the pills make me sleep, reopen old wounds. we are more
than the labels arbitrarily assigned to us. i swallow the salt.

i cannot say you did not warn me. i have always been susceptible
to beauty. your body is at the beginning of everything.
i look for a way out, pacing the halls. there are no exits
from inside oneself. the city has expanded to the size
of a small fishbowl. i swim back and forth.
you do not love me, but you love me.
 the universe is still expanding, and so am i—
so is this.

Thank You Poem
I hold an ember between two fingers. This week's theme is: disappointment. Do you know the specifics of extinguishment? You are as cold as a knife. I place my hand on your chest to listen for a heartbeat; finding none, I look elsewhere. How do we prove our humanity? I felt nothing when you kissed me. It felt good, that nothing. It felt like justice.

I look for love in all the wrong places. Under the bed, in the back of the closet. I pour the moon into a jar for you to keep on your back porch and distill. Thank you, you say but do not say. I don't know why I expected anything less.

It seems so easy now, to say: this is what happened. I sort through my feelings with a butter knife, cutting memories into even slices. You are a small fire. I rest my palms on your shoulders, trying to see if you are real, that I haven't imagined you; unable to prove anything, I look elsewhere. How do we assess reality? I felt nothing when you kissed me. It felt right, that nothing. It felt like justice.

I look for loss in all the wrong places. Behind the couch, under the fruit bowl. I catch the stars with my right hand and give them to you as a snack to eat on alternate side parking days. Thank you, you say but do not say. I don't know why I expected anything less.

I look for the means of escape, and find none. I am trapped in this world of four discreet walls. You are a sliver of ash. I beat my fists against your back in an attempt to hurt you; unable to make you feel anything, I look elsewhere. How can we make a new world out of the old one? I felt nothing when you kissed me. It felt cold, that nothing. It felt like justice.

13 hrs, 43 mn
short-circuit		small fry		break through
or breakdown?
	only time will tell.		the smell of liquor
on electronics.
coming down		from so high		has never hurt
so much.
	the higher you fly		the further you fall
or so they tell me.
i've never believed anyone		as much as i believe you.

you tell me to be nicer. i don't want nice, i want you to do what you do best: detachment.

long drive,		13hrs		43mn.		the space in
between		distance.
	you can't outrun			the Devil.
i try		to get ahead of you		with prosecco in
plastic cups
	cigarettes			outside on the lawn
	at night—
gold pack		white trim		the smell of cordite.

you tell me to be nicer. i don't want nice, i want you to do what you do best: cruelty.

soft skin		hard push		get away
from me.
	i need you like i need		a hole
in the head.

still, i feel it.   something magical
something bad
          about the way you tip your hat   the way you smoke my
cigarette
your belt buckle   glinting   in the
last light.

you tell me to be nicer. i don't want nice, i want you to do what you do best: break me.

Late Nights
You call me a punk—not an insult, a way of being. I have no desire for
violence.
The same sidewalks I scraped my knees on as a child have now become
the enemy.
Your tight jeans and Tennessee heat amuse me. You complain
About the lack of good drugs. What are we becoming?
We ask each other, afraid of the real answers.
Afraid of the truth.

I miss the way that with you, certain things become obvious. Others,
Completely obscure. You quote the Book of Job and guzzle whiskey.
I twist myself into a knot and try to explain Fitzgerald, Pretoria,
Anne Carson. The nature of love, trust, madness.
It gets late, dark.

 I can hear your voice in my ears, even now. We are partners in crime,
Trading blows and solidarities. I've always liked the way you laughed,
Even when something wasn't really funny.
Can you reach me now? Even as the moon comes out from between the
trees?
I reach out and find only the splendid blackness.

Prose Poem

My dopamine rush, your alienation from the real world, my red nails, your hair growing back out, my serotonin deficiency, your problematic essay due on the fifteenth, my tiresome questions that have always bothered you but which you answer anyway, humoring me, your philosophical wanderings through the metaphysical world, my catsup, your sense of humor, my fried eggs, your failed or aborted attempt at intimacy, my messed up sleep schedule, your weight gain which I think is absolutely adorable but you are uncomfortable with, my weight gain which you have yet to comment on, your body, my body, our bodies together, in conjunction with, but not necessarily connected to; each other. Do you understand what I mean by that?

Your lost tooth, my lost sense of being, your Johnnie Walker nights, my Budweiser days, my Marlboro men, your stealing drags right out of my mouth, my grabby hands and lipstick prints, your neck like an accusation, our hands holding one another's outside of that bar where we went to smoke that night in early February; it was just getting dark out, we were laughing, you were saying something funny, my stomach twisting, your hands on my back, my hands on your wrists, my bones heavier than lead, your eyes an uncanny shade of blue, I come back to this again and again; I don't know why.

No rest for the wicked: your sleepless nights, my sleepless days, we are getting restless, I am getting restless, the restlessness is getting restless, you take long drives and I take long walks, as if we were animals circling the limits of our cages, parakeets spreading our wings to take flight; my clipped wings, your limitless wingspan, miles and miles, I wonder how you fill your days, whiskey and rough sex, typewriters and Civil War era machinery, I have only one thing to say to you, perhaps it is the only story I will ever tell, once I might have had many stories, now I have only one.

In a strictly theoretical manner of speaking:
If God cannot make man in his image, why make man at all?
I want to break you down, then build you back up again. So far, you have proved
Unbreakable. I make up reasons why you should tell me your secrets,
Extended metaphors; but instead you go on long drives,
Sharpen your knives, and turn out the light on the porch
So I cannot find my way home
In the dark.
What I want is somehow inconsequential, secondary to what
You are capable of. I have always been here, always been fumbling
In the shallows. I stumble in the murk, tripping over myself
Looking for the pinprick in the darkness
Like a moth looking for a match.
You have always been the circle of light at the top of the stairs,
The adrenaline rush of a word held to the tongue and then unsaid.
I worry you'll see yourself in these pages.
Still, in between dreams and sleep I have to ask myself,
In a strictly theoretical manner of speaking:
If I cannot love you in my own way
Why love you at all?

the last smoking holdouts
i live for the tragic back-and-forth;
    we stay up too late, trading barbs,
drinking,
    the same kind of dishonest trickery you once employed
to get me into bed now keeps me up nights.

    me, one of the last
smoking holdouts;
    i struggle with affection for you. it squirms
in my chest.
    i want to cut it out of me. it has no use.
it only serves to make me miserable on sleepless days spent alone and
wanting.
    you presume to know me, but you cannot
        know this.

i want to reach through the screen
    and take hold of you by the collar. they say
        beauty is in the details, but i say
it is in the hollow of your collarbone. waiting is not
    something i do well.
just one more month, you say.

nudes
me, i grow more beautiful day by day
    sitting in the dark;
        a state of suspended animation

you accuse me of teasing you:

it makes me afraid, to think that you could possibly want me
    in any capacity

i just want you to see what you're missing, i say

i know the signs, the way you touch me
and yet i cannot believe it, that you
think about me in the dark.
that you reach for me
with fingertips burning
like lighted matches?

how do you understand
the desires of someone
else?

Proceed at your own risk
You are thinking of me late at night, calling; sing me a song. I'm the piano man. I wish you carried a warning label: proceed at your own risk. I read the papers, check my horoscope. There are no concrete reasons why I should distrust you; yet I do. I sow discord in between the syllables of your name, spin wild tales of bank robbers and Bonnie-and-Clyde in my fantasies. Yes, I would like to run away with you. A dream; a car; a fifth of whiskey in the glove box. Marlboros and matches. There is a certain magic in things that will never happen.

In my room alone, I swallow swords and count down the days left on my calendar. A year passes in stops and starts. The thought of you, thinking of me, is tantalizing. I want to be in your dreams, haunting your waking nightmares. You bring with you a certain anxiety. And I am thinking about the grace that comes with violence. Should I expect another call in the middle of the night? I ask, hopeful. Radio silence on the other end of the line.

cough
cough, clear out the lungs.
        i send smoke signals from brooklyn to your unincorporated
house
traveling at the speed of light—

and i feel dirty, as if i've broken some promise to you
    some promise you don't know i've made.
i like the taste of my own lips, coffee in the morning, blood in the water.

maybe we could, in some parallel world
    be poets together, write a new universe
        where the sun doesn't set or it always does.

you tell me you want to write something new.
    it'll come when it comes, i say.

the best ideas come at night. halfway dreaming, i fan the flames of sleep.

i get the most satisfaction from watching the sun move
    sitting outside, waiting for the next big thing;
the next revelation.

you are the revelation, in your black t-shirt and your sweat
    i am alive from wanting.

i could almost reach across time zones to touch your chest.
    i could almost leap over mountain ranges
cross rivers, highways, 7/11s on the side of the road
    to get you in your room with the shades pulled.

cough, clear out the lungs.
    my smoke signals get caught in the trees and dissipate.
do you hear me whisper your name in the dark?
    or does it get lost in that other universe

the one i've only dreamed of?

free association
jeff told me that poets are always smoking and i'm beginning to wonder if the punishment fits the crime

it's cloudy on a friday, is that supposed to mean something? i read somewhere that nothing happens for any reason, i'm likely to believe that

my mother talks a lot about alienation, she thinks we are separated from each other; she's very intuitive, my mother

according to quantum mechanics, the multiverse is uniquely set up for immortality

lobsters are technically immortal, but more likely to die when doing their molting, which i think is terribly ironic and sad: to grow is to die

i sit in the sun and imagine that you are tracing my tan lines with your tongue

they say you're never more than eight feet from a spider, and all i can say is, that's a lot of legs

i start small fires in the hopes that you will see one of them and notice me, this hasn't worked yet but i am optimistic

Part Four: Acceptance
(noun) the action of consenting to receive or undertake something offered.

"Contemplate the similarity between the phrases 'being patient' and 'being a patient'," —*An Unquiet Mind*, Kay Redfield Jamison

"Do the young still fall in love, or is that a mechanism obsolete by now, unnecessary, quaint, like steam locomotion?" —*Disgrace*, J.M. Coetzee

Fragments
1.
You tell me
I'm being difficult.

2.
I make eggs, burn myself on the pan. Poetic justice,
I tell myself.

3.
The last sunburn I had
Lasted two whole weeks.

4.
It's May, and it's not warm out
Yet. I sit outside anyway, praying
For rain.

5,
The Virgin watches over me, literally and figuratively.
She's on my back, blessing me
For better or worse.

6.
I get grass-stains on my ass and have to do laundry
For the third time this week.

7.
I don't miss you, but I miss your physical body. The taste
Of space.

8.
I want Divine Intervention, because what I'm doing now
Isn't working.

gift poem
i wanted to write you a love story   but we are not in love—
    and i don't tell stories   anymore.
    so i write this
instead.

i wish i knew all your secrets.   you affect me like a drug—
    i am less clever in your hands.   we will never sleep
near each other.   this is what they call
an absolute.
    close to you   i cannot relax.   instead i count
the straight razor
of your ribs.   the shape of you underneath
your shirt.
    the sweat   under your lip. wanting is something   i am
used to
but not like this.

i want to thank God   for being so thoughtful   when He
built you.
    i am not a believer.   this is what they call
mania.
it twists and burns   me into something new.
something cold.
    i fight it   with both hands.   i do not
always win.
you keep the cold at bay   with your sweat   your
heat.
    i am used to feeling   grateful   indebted
even

but not like this.

i want to see you again   but i don't know when   i will.
    longing is something   tangible. this is what they call   *loss.*
it rests in my chest.   you say we will
see each other again
    someday.   how soon   is soon?
    i want to know.
patience is a virtue.   you ask me to hold on   just a
little bit longer.
    i am waiting   for my bruises to heal. i am used to
feeling small
but not like this.

poem to be burned
if cleanliness is next to godliness,
    then, god help me, i want to be dirty. i am starting to dream in verse again,
like moses parting the red sea;
    when i wake up, the words have left me
        like a woman leaving the door unlocked. your holiness
can be proved by the long line from your throat
    to your collarbone;
        here i worship.

your body the altar
    i make my offering:
        not love, but something
  worse.
        you turn me down with a loose grin
    like a skeleton coming alive
        to see what he has missed.

i am afraid i only see you in sleep.
    you visit me in dreams, a burning bush
speaking with the voice of God.
    awake, you tell me i'm doing a better job of being kindly
        to you. i don't want softness, i want violence. i want it to
hurt;
i want fire to do what it does:
    burn—

a hand holding itself is a fist
clean now, i make a model of you
        out of the leftovers from dinner. blood and bone,
a small offering to God. and i want pain, bright and clear, more than
anything else.
        there exist certain things i cannot do to myself.

you are a wound
        i constantly reopen. i don't know why i love
to hurt myself this much. you keep me company late nights
        with the book of job on your tongue
and johnnie walker in a shot glass.
        i quote fitzgerald and fall asleep, wishing you
would touch me.

i wish i could kill the part of me
        that wants you. without it, i would be strong
again. i wash you out of my hair with hot water, prayer,
        and soap.

a woman standing alone
        is a message. a lie told twice is a promise.
a hand holding itself is a fist.

this modern psychosis
sundown, and it is starting to get cold again.
i count the days in birth control packets, tubes of lipstick
trips to the grocery store for beer or smokes.
was it only two months ago
when we pressed our bodies together
like parentheses closing a sentence?
i don't think in terms of time, just time
wasted.

i don't know what it is that makes me dwell.
these days, this modern psychosis
what the Greeks called "*genius*"
addles me.
i call the doctor, complaining
of hysteria. this madness
has your name written
all over it.

i miss you, but more than that
i miss sitting in that small room with glass walls,
wanting to want you, waiting
for you to close the immeasurable distance.
now we are separated by more than space.
i want you to come back
with your laugh like an accusation.
i want you to accuse me.

sunburnt
afternoon after the beach, and you were too sunburnt
for me to hold you. i've always thought
the best embraces hurt a little;
i've always liked to play with fire.
a little cruelty
goes a long way.

later, my burns faded to tan lines
and i went home, thousands of miles away
from you and your red shoulders,
your smile like a shard of light—

i only miss you very late at night, or early in the morning
when i remember sleeping next to you, waking up blurry and achy
to sunshine coming in through the blinds, tasting salt on your skin.
you slept with your back towards me, a constellation of freckles
i counted and named as you dreamed.

when i think about the time we wasted,
slow mornings with our limbs half-tangled,
the nights dancing to records spinning on the record player,
breaking open pill capsules just to feel something new,
i wonder if time is in fact the enemy, not distance.

with my eyes closed, i think about the burns, now faded. the sore spot
on my skull, which has now healed. there are never enough days
to do what we want. but still i have to ask:
who would we be? if we were close?

all i have to offer is my own confusion
i write one line for every day we stay separate. i am learning how to live without lipstick, learning how to be alone again. the milk has gone bad, the clocks have all stopped, still i wait for you like a limb waits to be reattached.

you, with your quotes and your bottles, the slim joy i get when i say your name. i draw lines on my eyelids in the hopes it will make you notice me. i am now defined on an axis of blood and bone; of need and want.

i toss small pebbles into the pond of my mind and watch the ripples. you have caused more waves than i would like to admit. you are a wound i constantly reopen; i pick at the edges of the scab and watch the blood pool.

i want to exorcise you from my being the way you would get rid of a demon. i sage the house, salt the doors, put a saucer of milk on the doorstep. i dye my hair red. why me? i ask God, as nicely as i can. God doesn't answer.

i take my medicine. you treat me as if i have answers that will unlock the door to the universe. i wonder what i did to convince you of any coherence. all i have to offer is my own confusion, i tell you, and take more pills until your face disappears from my mind for good.

Poker-Faced

The sun sets slower here. I cup it in my hands, let it pool through my fingers. We argue through screens all day, poker-faced. A quiet cacophony; I wonder what you would think of my innermost secrets. You say you're taking note: of what? Inquiring minds want to know. I worry you're catching wind of the lesser things. My needs, my wants.

A simple thing: a picture of the river. *Jump in and swim across*, you say. I bite back a smile; I miss your chaos. A system will always trend towards disorder, you remind me. What is the taxonomy of a wish?

Something like loss runs through me; like ice. You accuse me of being vague. Are you mad at me? I want to know. I could never handle you if you were angry. These modern vices have modern solutions. What's more important, the players, or the game? I worry you are catching on. You were always cleverer than you looked. Defeated, I turn my head away. I look at the moon.

existence is too enormous
he is in tennessee and losing his mind.
existence is too enormous, he says. i have half a mind
      to agree with him. i want to go back to sleeping under blue sheets
driving in the dark, walks along the river — we were like any other couple
           except with less *time*.

i am in new york and for once i have my wits about me.
       i am no longer brilliant. God is not speaking to me anymore.
a pity, but that's how it goes.

i want to help, but there is only so much a person can do. late nights, i stay up,
      waiting for his call. for drinking beer and wanting to touch,
for need. for waking dreams, memories of being held and held down.

he makes me feel contained. oh how i feel so uncontained—

existence is too enormous. we all need someone to pin us to the bed, to hold our wrists
      to press our bodies down with the weight of their own.
to make jokes and place cold beer bottles in our empty, waiting hands
      to teach us how to smoke a bowl with helpful thumbs moving in time.

he is in tennessee and losing his mind. i can't help him find it, just like he can't help
      me find mine when i am lost to the highs and lows.

Banging your head against a wall for one hour burns 150 calories
I miss you, and I can't figure out how to tell you how much I love the shape of your mouth when you say something cruel. We are no longer looking at the same moon; do you remember that day in October when it hung low and orange above the Myrtle subway tracks? I told you to look and you couldn't find it. I was with somebody else. Later, I planted kisses on your neck and you wiped them off in a smear of dark-red lipstick. I can't tell if my desire for you is genuine, or just a desire for something different. My days are all the same. My lower back aches. Down South, you drink your absinthe and complain to me about the state of the universe. I cannot help you stretch against the confines of your cage. The bars bend; they do not break.

we can only hold each other, across distance. we can only be voices on the phone,
hoarse and slightly sweet,
      calling at all hours of the night.

when my pipeline to God opens back up again, dear
      i'll make sure to ask him:
why are we like this?

      existence is too enormous, he says.

Inertia
I know why I like you; you have velocity. Almost terminal,
You do less speed now but you still have that animal quality;
That hush. That rush;
I count days in text messages, your green voice
Bubbling up from the depths of my psyche to torture me
With hard questions. What is the precise shape
Of the universe? A curved ball
Or more like a disc?
I trip over my own tongue trying to please you. You are clinical in your observations,
Poker-chipped. You undress me with the exactitude of a surgeon
Preparing his next meal. Your voice the sharp monotone of someone
Who has done too many amphetamines. I love your hard flat laugh;
Whiskey-hoarse you quote someone I've never heard of
And swallow shots. I smoke like an unhappy chimney and placate you
With what I have left of myself.
You have never promised me any act of mercy. What would that look like? I want to know. Whatever invincibility I had is long gone. I am at your disposal, your knife at my throat. You move at a different speed than I do; an object in motion tends to stay in motion. I hitch my wagon to your star, hoping to go faster, faster. This is a mistake; I cannot change my natural orbit.
I spin out, your hands pinning my wrists behind my back in a spasm of desire. An object at rest tends to stay at rest. Wanting more,
Always wanting more, but never getting it—
I fold, and collapse back into myself.

on not loving you
not being in love feels like a joke someone has played on me. my whole life,
i've been in love with someone or another. now i'm trying to be in love with you; it's not working.
    you can try, you just can't force the boat to dock
in the ferry station. i do want you, want you like i want thunderstorms to wash away all the cigarette butts i've left on the stoop of my apartment building
    like i want red dresses on sundays and hollow cheekbones and lucid dreaming
but want is different than love.
want is a lit match at the base of your spine, a lung ache,
    the stem of a broken wine glass. it is your chest, heaving with exertion.
i do not even get relief in sleep. all my dreams have to do with cages.
    want has become a way of being. it propels me forward. i use my desire for you to get through the day.
    if i'm not in love with you, then what am i?
    you have become somehow necessary to the process. want is the distance between us, not easily closed.
    i reach out with both hands, find space between my fingertips, but i will not
stop reaching.

there will be blood
do your parents know what you get up to in that room upstairs?
i know i am not as beautiful as i used to be. still, you seem
       to want me. at my core, i want to be wanted
exclusively. do you know
 i would do anything
       you told me to do? these random acts of violence
are a part of my education. you call our union
       bittersweet, say i am needlessly defensive
you are genuine—surreptitious, maybe—but genuine.
       i have a hard time believing anything you have ever said or done.
i doubt you are aware of the depths of my devotion to the cause.
       the night is dangerous;
the truth comes out in the dark. you use your teeth, a knife
whatever gets the job done. i want to reach through the screen,
       i want you to bruise me.
sometimes we devour each other. not often enough,
you say. and i am begging you to come back—
       maybe, you say. maybe.

What is fear afraid of?
Five years, and I am surprised by the absence of brutality. Why do we have to live in our bodies? I do not know how to talk about what I want. I try to interpret the signals you've sent me and find only hieroglyphics. Your face: an assault. I look at what we've built and it shakes me.

I try to be tender and fumble with my lines. You aren't the easiest person to know, or love. Why do we have to live in our bodies? The back of my hand is suddenly fascinating.

What is fear afraid of? You are a benevolent God. Even when you are ridiculing me, the shape of your jaw thrills me.

We are all sinners. I worry daily about being caught red-handed. You start drinking early, smoothing the ripples in the water. I am struggling to hold onto my sanity, like a woman trying not to fall asleep. What I need is the need itself. Hair knotted back, I need you to pull.

smoking poem
smoking alone is different from smoking with someone else.
nine o' clock, and i am wishing for your hands,
on my hands, i am wishing for your smoke. i am wishing to be outside
of the bar, smoking
with you making hands for my cigarette. it even tastes different,
the time difference, you saying
"just give me the last drag, let me kill it,"
and i would let you kill me
just for one more night
outside in the summer, your feet in your flip-flops,
tight jeans, belt buckle shining
like a gun in the neon light. it's finally getting hot
i cannot sleep for sweating
and wanting you, my chest hurts
from the chain smoking, from needing you
to be here in this city like a fallen star.
i am getting used to distance.
smoking alone is like the beat of solitude,
the cough that clears out the lungs, it has a specific taste
i want to press my tongue against the flat of your chest.
instead i go outside yet again, taking my hard pack and lighter
changing all the time,
becoming a new creature,
someone who can smoke alone
someone who can be alone
without you.

light a match
you are a punch to the gut
       a revelation
i talk to God. he says, yes, *do it*
       take that train, run faster, throw it all away for love.
what we have is not what i would call *typical.*
       you standing up to take off your tight jeans,
me in my matrix coat and red lipstick. heels click on the pavement as i click
       away from you. light a match and watch it
burn.

you are a cigarette burn on the underside of an arm
       a red stain in white flesh.
i talk to God. he says, yes, *do it*
       burn it down, take that plane, throw it all away for love. what we have is not
what i would call *normal.*
       you making grabby hands for my pack of smokes,
me leaving my lip prints on the skin of your neck. i know you hate me,
       hate that you want me,
hate the way i have marked you. light a match and watch it
       burn.

you are a slap in the face
       an offering to the deities
i talk to God. he says, yes, *do it*
       crush that angel between the palms of your hands. throw it all away for love.
what we have is not what i would call *healthy.* you kicking off your boots

      in my small room, leaving them neatly at the foot
of my bed. me saying *honey* like it's the last word to ever be said. i know i want you,
      want you to want me, want us to want everything. want to be dissolved
in a bath of want. light a match and watch it burn
      everything.